Traditions Around The World
Masks

by Amanda Earl and Danielle Sensier

Thomson Learning
New York

Traditions Around The World

Books in this series:

Costumes

Masks

Cover: A *tatanua* mask from the Pacific.

Consultant: Anthony Shelton, Keeper of Non-Western Art and Anthropology, Royal Pavilion Art Gallery and Museums, Brighton, East Sussex, England.

First published in the
United States in 1995 by
Thomson Learning
115 Fifth Avenue
New York, NY 10003

First published in Great Britain in 1994 by
Wayland (Publishers) Ltd.

Library of Congress Cataloging-in-Publication Data
Earl, Amanda.
  Masks/by Amanda Earl and Danielle Sensier.
     p.   cm.—(Traditions around the world)
  Includes bibliographical references (p.   ) and index.
  ISBN 1-56847-226-9
  1. Masks—Social aspects—Juvenile literature. [1. Masks]
I. Sensier, Danielle. II. Title. III. Series
GT1747.E25   1994
391'.434—dc20   94-20748

Printed in Italy

Picture acknowledgments:

The publishers wish to thank the following for providing the photographs for this book: Brighton Museum and Art Gallery 34; © British Museum 40, 45; Bruce Coleman Limited *cover,* 14-15, 16, 17, 18 and 19 (Frans Lanting), 28-29 (Norman Myers) 40-41, 44-45; Robert Estall 39 (© Angela Fisher); Explorer 12, 37; Eye Ubiquitous 8 (© Eric Enstone), 28, 43; The Hutchison Library 10-11, 26-27, 27, 29, 35; Life File 11 (Jeremy Hoare), 14 (Sally-Ann Fison), 23 (Richard Powers), 24 (Jeremy Hoare); Link 15, 25 (Lourdes Grobet)and 32; Tony Morrison 6-7, 21 (© Tony Morrison), 20-21, 22, 25; Edward Parker 6; Photri 30-31; Still Pictures 34-35, 36, 38-39; Rock Graphics 38; Tony Stone Worldwide 8-9; Tropix 42-43 (M. Jory).

Artwork by Peter Bull.

Contents

Masks around the world

NORTH AMERICA

SOUTH AMERICA

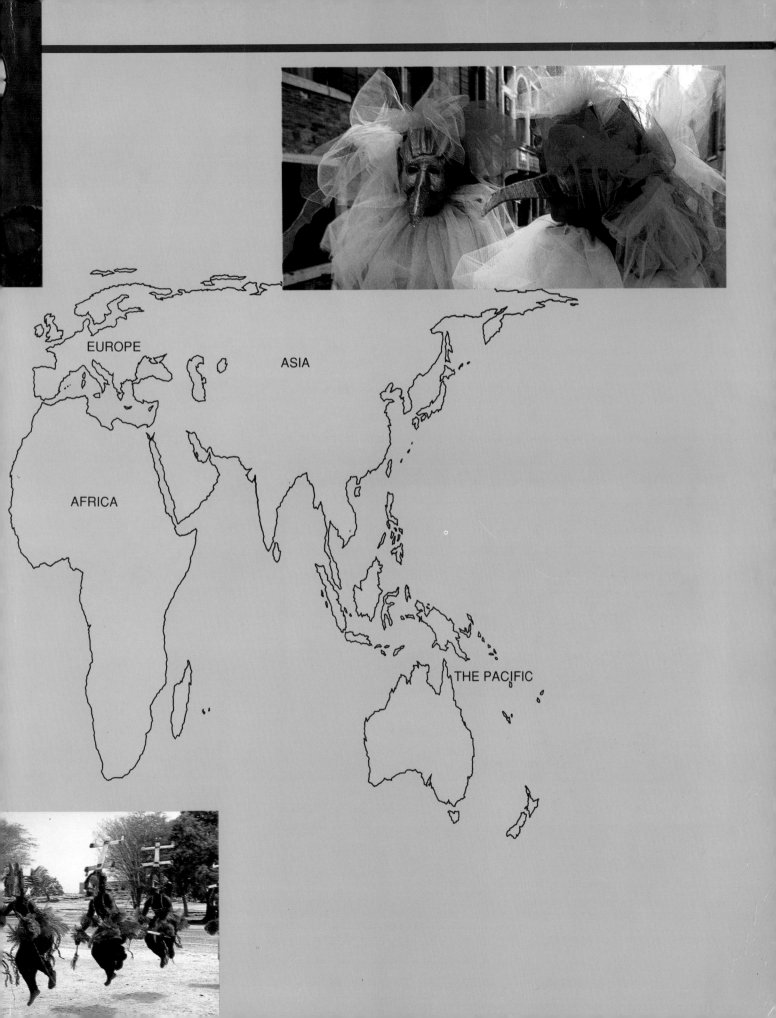

EUROPE

ASIA

AFRICA

THE PACIFIC

Introduction

Masks play an important part in many different traditions around the world. When people put on masks they are usually disguising themselves, and can almost feel they have become other persons, or animals, ghosts, or whatever the mask represents. In fact, in some religions it is believed that the wearer actually changes into a spirit or ancestor.

Masks are sometimes worn for fun at costume parties or at Halloween. At other times they are used in the theater to help audiences identify different characters. In many parts of the world where carnivals and festivals are very popular, colorful masquerades are an important part of the celebrations.

For some people, masks are an essential part of their beliefs and customs. Elaborate masks are worn at religious ceremonies to mark an important event. This might be to celebrate a successful harvest, to appeal to spirits for rain, or at an initiation ceremony, when a child is ready to become an adult.

An African mask. ▶

**Main picture:
In Central and South America, masks are worn at religious festivals and masquerades. At this market stall in Guatemala, a great variety of masks are for sale, representing ancestors, animal spirits, and demons.**

6

▲ **A theatrical dance mask from Bali, Indonesia. This is Rangda, an evil character from the Barong dance dramas.**

People have used masks for many thousands of years. The oldest known mask, representing a coyote, was found in Mexico and is about 10,000 years old. Other masks found by archaeologists are from ancient Egyptian times, when masks were made for the mummified bodies of the dead.

Mask designs reflect the traditional arts and crafts of the region in which they are made. They can have many different forms – animal, human, or a mixture of both – and a variety of colors, textures and patterns.

Masks are usually made from the kinds of natural materials that are easy to find locally. They vary from region to region, and range from barkcloth in Papua New Guinea to cowrie shells and feathers in Zaire. Today's mask makers also use manufactured materials, such as light bulbs and rubber tubing.

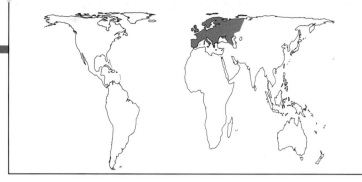

Europe

Europe has many exciting masking traditions, usually linked to the changing of the seasons, religious celebrations, or theatrical performances. In ancient Greek theater, actors sometimes wore masks, and during the Renaissance, masks became fashionable at extravagant masked balls held by the European aristocracy. The famous masked carnival in Venice, Italy, has been celebrated since medieval times. However, not all European masquerades have had such a long history. The Notting Hill Carnival in London was started in the 1960s by Afro-Caribbean people who had migrated to England.

Many masquerades in Great Britain mark the changes of the seasons. In parts of Oxfordshire, Gloucestershire, and Scotland, mumming plays are performed around Christmastime. *Mumming* comes

Main picture: At the Venice Carnival, the streets are filled with people wearing richly decorated masks. These are often worn as part of an extravagant costume.

In Cornwall, England, ▶ the beginning of the summer is celebrated at the Padstow Hobby Horse masquerade. This fearsome monster dances through the streets shouting "Summer is a-come today."

from the German word for mask, and mummers, or "guisers" in Scotland, have to make sure nobody knows who they are. Each performer wears a hat that has long strips of newspaper coming down over the face, and a costume also covered with strips. In the dance an "old man" is "killed," symbolizing winter's end and the beginning of spring.

In the Welsh counties of Mid Glamorgan and Dyfed, the end of summer is marked with the *Mari Lywd* processions held in December and January. A masked figure, covered totally by canvas, carrying a carved horse's head on a pole, is a well-known visitor. The carved wooden mask has a snapping mouth and green glass eyes.

◀ An ugly witch mask from the *Schemenlaufen* Festival in Austria. Masks are worn to scare away winter and bring a good harvest.

At the Notting Hill Carnival in London, thousands ▶ of people perform dances, music, and masquerades, known as *mas'*. Each *mas'* group has its own theme, which is changed every year. Stunning costumes and masks are skillfully crafted, following themes such as "our arrival," "colors of the rainbow," and "birds of paradise."

In Scotland, the history of the masked Burry Man of South Queensferry dates back to the 1740s. This strange figure is covered from head to foot with sticky green burrs from the burdock plant. Thousands of burrs are collected and attached to a loosely-woven material, which is then modeled into a close-fitting mask and costume. The mask is crowned with a huge hat covered with seventy red roses. It is believed the tradition is somehow linked to the safety of fishing fleets on their journeys.

In the *Silvesterkläuse* festival in Urnasch, Switzerland, masked "spirits of the New Year" go from house to house visiting people. It is thought the masked tradition was once a way of begging in disguise. It has now turned into a festival for people to show off their stunning masks and craft skills. There are three groups of masked figures: the *schöne* (the beautiful), the *wüeschte* (the ugly), and the *schö-wüeschte* (the less ugly). The masks represent men and women, but they are very heavy, so they are only worn by men.

Austria's best-known masked festival is the *Schemenlaufen*. In medieval times, masked figures chased bad spirits away to make sure there was a good harvest. The festival is still held every three years in the town of Imst.

Strange and wonderful animal masks are popular in parts of Eastern Europe. In Poland, the *Turon* mask is worn at harvest and fertility rituals held by farmers. The mask is named after a creature from Polish folk tales and is covered with animal skin, goat or ram horns, and shiny metal disks for eyes. It is a hobbyhorse and is held on a pole, the person carrying it being disguised by a huge shroud of material. It has a large hinged mouth that snaps open and shut when a cord is pulled. In Bulgaria, fox, bear, and bird masks are worn at new year celebrations, which in the past were linked with the start of the new sowing and harvesting season. At the celebrations, masked animal figures have to jump high in the air, since in earlier years it was believed the crops would grow as high as the highest jump.

11

Some of the most varied and beautifully crafted masks can be found at the Venetian Carnival in Italy. Along with processions of gondolas and sideshows of every kind, thousands of Venetians and visitors alike join in this huge masquerade. The festivities go on for seven days, and date back to a lively, fun-filled medieval festival that took place just before the religious period of Lent, when people fasted for forty days. In fact, the words *carne vale* are the Latin words for "farewell to meat."

Venice becomes a big, open theater, where people choose from a variety of masks and act as they please because their identity is hidden. There are *gnaghe* masks, which men wear to disguise themselves as women. Another of the favorite disguises is the *bautta* mask with its tricorn (three-cornered) hat.

This mask is a black or white half-mask which is worn with a long cloak. In the past it was meant to be worn only by certain noblemen, but on one particular day it could be worn by both rich and poor alike. The plague-doctor mask, with its long, hooked nose, is worn with special clothes that were once thought to protect the wearer from the plague.

Masks are still used in Europe in some theatrical performances, including pantomimes. Pantomime masks are lots of fun, and are usually worn by the frightening characters, such as the giant Blunder Bore from *Jack the Giant-Killer*. In today's performances of Shakespeare's plays such as *Much Ado About Nothing* and *A Midsummer Night's Dream*, masks are worn to disguise the characters, with comic results.

Project : Making a Venetian Carnival mask

You will need:
Large, old plastic bowl
Old newspapers (4 sheets)
Water
White glue
Cardboard box
Pencil
Scissors
Elastic
Paints
Paintbrushes

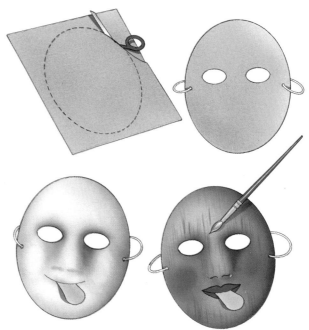

1 Tear up old newspaper into small pieces (about the size of a postage stamp), and place in a bowl. Soak the newspaper overnight in water.

2 Mash up the newspaper so it looks like wet bread. Pour and then squeeze out as much of the water as you can. Add some glue and mix together, keeping the mixture fairly dry. This is now papier mâché.

3 On your cardboard, draw an oval shape the size of your face and cut it out. Cut eyeholes, and pierce holes on either side of the mask with the scissors to thread the elastic through. Then build up the features on your mask with papier-mâché: a fat nose, bulging cheeks, and perhaps a wart or a boil. Cover the cardboard completely with papier-mâché and allow it to dry in a warm place.

4 Paint your mask to make it look as if it were carved from wood, adding the grain of the wood, as well as color to the lips and cheeks.

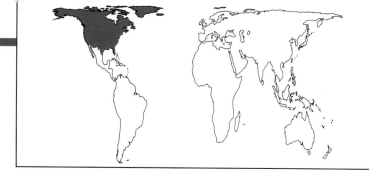

North America

In North America the most familiar masks are probably those worn at Halloween, a popular time for mischief, fun, and games. This festival dates back to the ancient Celts, who made human sacrifices to their gods at this time of year. Christians turned it into All Hallows' Eve, a frightening night when witches and devils were thought to walk the earth. It was introduced into the United States by British migrants in the eighteenth century. Today, all over the United States and Canada, people still disguise themselves as ghosts, witches, and monsters. Children dress up for "trick or treat," collecting candy from neighbors in exchange for not playing tricks.

These children are wearing ▶ modern, mass-produced skeleton masks. They are celebrating Halloween. They are carrying trick-or-treat bags for collecting candy.

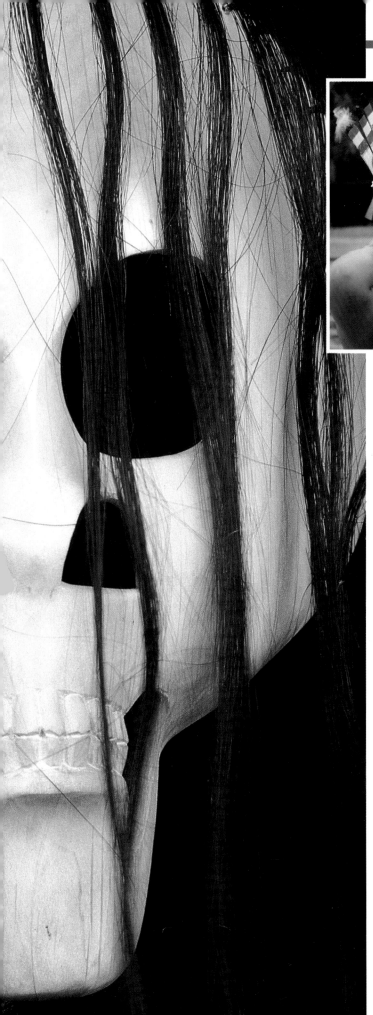

▲ Traditional Native American masks are still worn today. These feather and cloth masks are from New Mexico.

◄ This ghost monster mask from Vancouver Island, British Columbia, Canada, also looks like a skeleton. Hair has been attached to the mask to make it more realistic.

Long before the first migrants arrived in North America, Native Americans had their own masking traditions. Unfortunately, few of these have survived, since in the eighteenth and nineteenth centuries many Native Americans were killed or forced to abandon their lands and traditions. However, some now make and sell masks to tourists, helping to keep old skills alive as well as to earn money. In the Pacific Northwest, groups such as the Kwakiutl are performing their masquerades once again.

A carved and painted ▶ eagle-spirit mask, made by the Haida people of the Pacific Northwest.

The Hopi are one of the Native American peoples of the Rio Grande. They now live mostly in villages on the Hopi Reservation in Arizona. They make money from raising cattle and sheep, tourism, and arts and crafts, but they were traditionally crop farmers. This can be seen in their masquerades, which are linked to the sun and rain, a successful harvest, and the change of the seasons throughout the year.

Hopi *Kachina* masks are worn at dance ceremonies, such as the Bean and Water Serpent ceremonies in the spring and the Home Dance ceremony in the summer. The masks represent mythical spirits that help the Hopi to summon rain. When a dancer wears a *Kachina* mask, he doesn't just look like the spirit, he believes that he actually becomes the spirit.

Today, the *Kachina* masks are usually helmet-shaped and are made of leather or hide, with an added framework of plywood for attaching ears, noses, snouts, horns, and feather headdresses. Some are decorated with painted symbols such as budding corn, the sun, rain clouds, and a rainbow. Others represent humans, such as hunters, girl warriors, or grandmothers.

Along the coast of the Pacific Northwest, from Washington State up to Yakutat Bay in Alaska, mask-making is still flourishing among local artists, although traditional Native American lifestyles have almost disappeared. Groups used to be divided into separate clans, each with their own masks given to them by mythical ancestors. These were signs of the clan's authority, similar to European coats of arms. Many represented brave animal spirits, like the feathered eagle mask of the Nootka people. However, clans also honored creatures such as the mouse, frog, and woodworm. The masks were worn at *potlatch* feasts, where the more noble the clan, the more numerous were the masks.

16

The thunderbird mask of the Kwakiutl people belongs to the *Hamatsa* clan. It represents a frightening forest spirit that assists the mythical cannibal monster, *Bakbakwal-anooksiwae*. As with many Kwakiutl masks, it has special moving parts that are operated by the dancer wearing it. The mask measures up to 8 feet long and has a huge beak that can be snapped open and shut using pulleys and cords. It is carved from red cedar wood with fringes of cedar bark or animal skin.

After contact with outside traders, some Native American peoples began making masks to sell to European settlers. The Haida people were known for such masks, which were like portraits of real people. They even included carved moustaches, wrinkles, and European beards and hairstyles.

On the other side of the continent, in the east, the carved wooden masks of the False Face Society are still worn among some of the Iroquois peoples. False Face masks are believed to prevent and cure illness, their power coming from the first False Face spirit, the Great Doctor. He is said to have broken his nose in a contest with the Creator of the World, and so False Face masks have a twisted look of pain. As a result of losing the contest, he was ordered to rid the earth of disease. So masks carved in his image and hung with tiny bags of tobacco are said to have the power of healing – but only for ailments of the head area, such as nosebleeds and earaches.

False Face ceremonies involve masked dancing, prayers, and the burning of tobacco offerings. There are many rules about how False Face masks should be stored. If hung on a wall, a mask should always be covered or it may bring death. If it is not given regular offerings of tobacco, it is thought to bring bad luck; and if sold, it may come back to haunt its former owner. Some Iroquois believe that a fire in the New York State Museum in Albany, New York, in 1911 was caused by the museum's not providing regular tobacco to the masks in its care.

◀ **This Kwakiutl eagle mask is another mythical spirit figure. It is made of carved wood, and it has bird feathers to make it more like an eagle.**

◀ Today's Native American artists still make wooden masks. This bird mask is being carved from a single piece of wood. It will be painted with traditional designs and will take many hours to complete.

In the harsh Arctic region, the Inuit people once performed masquerades during the long winter months. Although present-day Inuits are now mainly Christian, respect for the natural world is still very important, and traditional ideas still influence their way of life. They believe everything in the universe has its own spirit, called *inua*. Inuit masks represent these many different spirits, such as the sun and moon, giant animals, or strange human beings. Several may be combined in one mask. Inuit masking traditions were also linked with hunting rituals. Each mask had its own special dance movements, performed to please the spirits of hunted animals.

Inuit masks are traditionally carved from driftwood, using beaver teeth and caribou antlers as tools. Many are surrounded by a band of wood with holes at the edge for attaching anything that shakes and rattles, such as feathers, small wooden pendants, whalebone, or even strips of animal intestine. There were also female finger masks, which women wore on their hands during dance ceremonies. The masks had round faces, eyes, teeth, and hair and were moved like puppets.

Traditional colors for masks were white, black, red, and blue. Before contact with European traders, the Inuit used natural pigments from sources such as white clay, swamp grass, and alder bark soaked in urine.

Today the Inuit do not follow masking traditions as they once did, although in the Nome area of Alaska masks are still made to entertain tourists. In other parts of the region, local artists sell their carvings to city museums and art galleries, a trade that is becoming an important way for the Inuit to earn money.

Project: Making a Kwakiutl bird mask

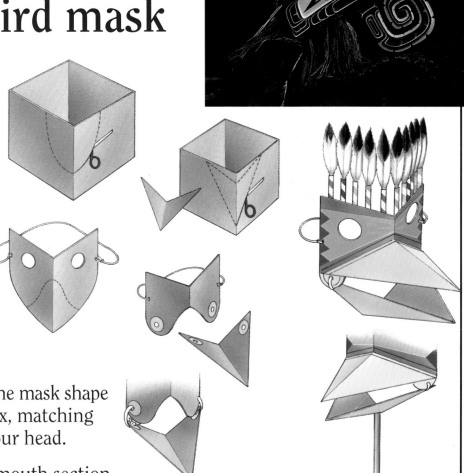

You will need:
Large cardboard box
Pencil
Ruler
Scissors
Elastic
Compass
Masking tape
Ribbon
Paints
Colorful drinking straws
Feathers
12-inch dowel rod

1 Draw and then cut out the mask shape using the corner of the box, matching the width and length of your head.

2 Cut away the nose and mouth section, and cut out eyeholes. Pierce small holes at the sides and attach a piece of elastic to hold the mask on.

3 Draw and cut out the upper beak using another corner of the box, and do the same for the lower beak, making it smaller.

4 Using the compass, draw four circles: two at the bottom ends of the face mask and two at each side of the lower beak where it will join the mask. Cover all four circles with a few pieces of masking tape (to reinforce the cardboard), and pierce a hole through the center of each circle.

5 Cut two strips of ribbon and thread each one through the matching holes. Tie a large knot at each end to keep the ribbon from pulling through. This is the moving part of the beak.

6 Use the masking tape to attach the top beak to the mask. Paint the beak and the face of the mask in bands of bright colors. Stick straws behind the top of the mask and add feathers at intervals.

7 Attach the dowel rod to the bottom of the lower beak with masking tape, so that you can move the beak up and down.

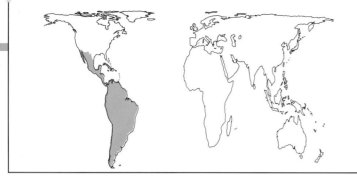

Central and South America

The masks of Central and South America have a very long history. Archaeologists believe they have existed since about 400 B.C. – 2,000 years before the Spanish conquests in the early sixteenth century. Many have been linked to the continent's ancient civilizations, such as the Aztecs of Mexico and the Incas of Peru. Rare Aztec masks of turquoise mosaic were found after the conquests, as well as decorated pottery showing masked figures at burial ceremonies.

Today, masking traditions are still widespread. Many are influenced by the beliefs of Amerindian peoples, who are the direct descendants of these ancient civilizations. Despite the near destruction of their race during the harsh colonial period, Amerindian peoples have survived and many are still living in the Andes and Mexico, as well as in remote areas of the Amazon Basin. They have strong beliefs in the power of nature, and masking traditions are an important part of these beliefs. Animals, plants, and the elements (such as rain and wind) are all thought to contain ancestors' spirits and other powerful spirits. Masks are worn to represent these spirits at ceremonies where people ask for help or try to please them with songs, dances, and gifts.

One of Bolivia's many elaborate devil masks. ▶

20

The masks of the Tucuna people in northern Brazil are worn in male and female initiation rituals. These take place when Tucuna children are ready to become adults. The wearing of Amerindian masks is usually restricted to men, but in this tradition they are also worn by girls and young women. Groups of masked dancers gather in the forest, returning to the house of their host to sing, dance, and enjoy a big feast. When the ritual is over, the masks become gifts to the initiated girl. All the masks represent strange animals and demons thought up by the person who made them, who is believed to be in communication with spirits or ancestors. Instead of being painted, the eyes are sometimes made of metal sheets, and the masks are fitted with false teeth made of tin.

A stunning gold sun-god mask from the ancient Inca civilization of Peru. ▼

Controlling people's actions was another purpose of Amerindian masks, such as those of the Tierra del Fuego Indians who once lived in the southern-most region of Argentina. Men wore masks to represent spirits who were thought to frighten women and make them obedient to men. An ancient legend told of a time when women made the rules and used masks to frighten men. Men were afraid of this power, so they performed the dance so that women would not gain control again.

Amerindian customs and beliefs have a strong influence on the masking traditions of Hispanic people living throughout the continent. Many of these people are of mixed race, descended from European settlers who took Amerindian wives during the colonial period. Although masks are worn during Christian festivals introduced by Europeans, many of the celebrations still reflect Amerindian beliefs.

Spanish priests, who arrived with the first settlers in the sixteenth century, did not approve of native traditions involving the masks of spirits and ancestors. They forced the Amerindians to adopt Christian festivals, and their masks were given horns and renamed "devils." In Bolivia, painted devil masks are worn by the tin miners of Oruro, in honor of their favorite Christian saint, the Virgin of Socavon, who is thought to have banished the devil from the community. The fierce-looking masks can be made from carved wood or factory-produced materials such as rubber tubing and electric light bulbs.

A Guatemalan dancer dressed ▶ up as a Spanish conquistador. Every year thousands of masked dancers act out scenes from the Spanish invasion of the early sixteenth century.

▲ One of Mexico's many festival masks, which are usually worn at religious celebrations. Notice the huge horns decorated with ribbons. With the introduction of Christianity, horns were added to many Amerindian masks to make them represent devils.

European-style masks are worn in dramatic masquerades such as the masked Dances of the Conquista, which tell of the first meetings between the Spanish conquistadors and Amerindian leaders. In Guatemala, these dancers wear realistic wooden face masks of the conqueror Pedro de Alvarado and the native leader, Tecum Uman, as well as of supporting characters such as soldiers and bulls.

In Mexico, most masquerades take place on saints' days or during carnival celebrations. They are also worn by wrestlers with imaginative names like "Atlantis" and "Aztec Eagle." Skull and devil masks are worn during the Day of the Dead festival when, once a year, dead souls are thought to return to the world. Children play with toy masks of painted papier-mâché, and there are also masked dances.

The masks of animal spirits are sometimes made more realistic by adding animal hair, bone, skin, or leather, and they often represent water-loving animals such as alligators, fish, and serpents. These masks are linked to rain ceremonies, which are very important in many areas of Central America. The Nahua people now wear these masks in Christmas processions, when the animal kingdom is said to worship the infant Jesus. At the same time, some of the ancient meaning still remains: the leading mask is a bat, considered by the Nahua to be the lord

Everybody joins in the Mexican Day of ▶ the Dead celebrations around November 1. In the villages, simple skeleton masks and traditional hats are worn by groups of dancers.

▲ A spectacular mask-float from the Rio de Janeiro Carnival, constructed from metal pipes and cogs.

of all animals, because it lives in caves, which are an important source of fresh water.

In countries all over the continent, masks are worn above all for fun and entertainment, and nowhere are they more lively than at Rio de Janeiro's Mardi Gras carnival in Brazil. This celebration is related historically to the European festivals held before Lent. It is the largest of its kind in the world, involving thousands of people in nonstop dancing and music. People wear fantastic masks and costumes, and high above the crowds the streets are decorated with huge clown and devil masks attached to lampposts.

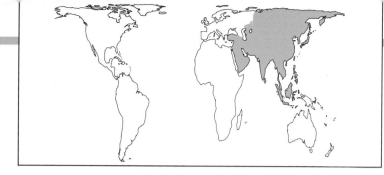

Asia

The variety of masks in Asia reflects the many religions and cultures in its countries. Masks are worn in harvest festival ceremonies in Borneo, "curing" ceremonies in Sri Lanka, and the Toraja peoples of Sulawesi use funeral masks called *pemia*. Yet Asia is probably best known for its stunning theatrical masks. Japan, India, Thailand, Java, and Bali all have their own forms of dance-dramas, and masks are an important part of performers' costumes.

The masks worn in a type of Japanese drama called No are realistic face masks resembling people, spirits, and mythical characters. There are five main types of masks: men, women, madmen, gods, and demons. The masks help the actors show their characters' feelings to the audience, from affection and passion to anger and cruelty. The skin tones of the mask, the hairstyle, and the shape of the mouth and teeth differ from character to character. One of the best-known masks is of a young woman, Ko-Omote, who is said to be the ideal of Japanese beauty. It has a pale, whitened face, straight black hair, and red lips. Even today, these masks are made with traditional materials. The carved wood is covered with *gofun* (powdered shell) and is painted with Chinese inks and natural dyes.

The masks worn in ▶ Japanese No dramas help the audience to understand the personality and feelings of each character.

▲ In the larger cities of India, masked *Ramlila* plays are watched by thousands of people in the streets. Each night a new scene is acted out. The last scene portrays the battle between Rama with his monkey army, and the demons led by Ravana.

The historical epic Hindu stories from India, the *Mahabharata* and the *Ramayana,* have had a great influence on masking traditions in Asia. Scenes from the stories are performed in many different masked dramas throughout the region, and not just in India. In India itself, the stories of the hero Rama and his wife Sita, who is captured by Ravana, are popular. Krishna's battles with demons are also acted out, and the god Vishnu appears as Narasinha, in the form of half-man and half-lion. The masked Ganesha, who has the head of an elephant and a small human body, usually appears at the beginning of each play, since he is believed to bring good luck during the performance.

Indian theatrical masks are either made from wood that is easy to carve or modeled in paper and glue, which is placed layer upon layer over a clay mold. Both types of masks are painted with bright colors, including gold and silver, and are then varnished. Mask makers usually follow set rules when making a mask, and they are forbidden to eat certain foods or drink alcohol.

Religious *lama* plays are part of an eight-day festival in Katmandu, the capital of Nepal. The Nepalese give thanks to the goddess Durga who is believed to help them farm their crops. One of the Durga masks has a crown, and tall poles with flags are attached to the crown in a huge fan shape. The mask can weigh as much as 22 pounds. In west Bengal, masks of the goddess Durga are also seen in *Chau* dramas. Here, the fan headdress is made of materials such as tinsel, glass beads, foil, and feathers.

▲ **A mask maker from Bali, carving one of the many masks used in the Barong dance dramas.**

The stories of the Barong dance dramas from Bali, Indonesia, are also based on the *Ramanyana,* especially the battle between Barong and Rangda. The fantastic wooden masks are brightly painted with bulging eyes. Barong, who is mischievous, usually appears in a dragon, cow, or tiger mask. Rangda, who

◀ Rangda is one of Asia's most evil dramatic characters. The tangled hair, fangs, and "fiery" tongue make this a really frightening mask.

▲ These papier-mâché masks from Thailand's *Khon* dramas are richly decorated to match the costumes.

is evil, has a mask with fangs, a long, floppy tongue, and tangled hair. The tongue, made from a long piece of red cloth, is decorated with gold leather flames. The mask is worn by one man, with the other performers acting as the back legs, similar to the two-man horse seen in the United States.

Some of the most exotic masks of Southeast Asia are found in Thailand's *Khon* dramas. All the roles, except those of the main heroines, are played by men. While the heroines wear just makeup on their faces, the men get to wear spectacular masks. The masks are made from papier-mâché, and the tall headdresses are carved from wood. The demon masks are usually painted gold, with beautiful greens and reds, and are decorated with tiny mirrors, colored glass, and mother-of-pearl.

Sri Lanka is well known for its "curing" masks. According to tradition, certain evil spirits cause different ailments. Today, ritual ceremonies called *sanni yakuma* are performed with dancers wearing wooden *sanni* masks. There are about eighteen different types of masks, each for a spirit responsible for an ailment, such as fever, shivering, or deafness. The mask for vomiting is blue and has a crooked mouth and squashed nose. The sick person is placed at the center of the masquerade, and the disease is believed to be driven from the body when he or she sees the masked "spirit."

In Borneo, harvest festival masks, called *Hudo* masks, are worn during a dance feast of the Dayak peoples, who live in the rain forests and on the southern coast. Rice is the main food of the Dayaks, and there are several ceremonies connected with the sowing, growing, and harvesting of the crop. *Hudo* masked dances are seen as a way of protecting the newly sown rice from evil spirits. The human, animal, bird, monkey, and crocodile masks worn during the dances have large eyes, and some have ears like butterfly wings or large earrings.

In Sri Lanka, the color of masks is very ▲ **important; light colors represent wealthy characters, and reds and greens are for demons.**

30

Children are sometimes included in the making and wearing of masks in Asia. Chinese people, particularly from Hong Kong, celebrate their new year with long festivities. Each Chinese year is named after a particular animal, such as the rat, the hare, or the pig. Children join in the fun at the new year by wearing masks of that year's animal. Children in Madhya Pradesh in India make masks from the skins of large fruits called gourds, which they wear at the popular children's *Cherta* festival. They have large slots for eyes and the teeth are made from grains of rice.

Project: Making a Durga Mask

You will need:
Large, stiff cardboard box
Pencil
Scissors
Paints
Paintbrushes
Tinfoil
Elastic
5 thin dowel rods, 8 inches long
Masking tape
Glitter
Silver tinsel
Glue
Shells
Recycled items: milk-bottle tops, crumpled magazine paper, small yogurt containers

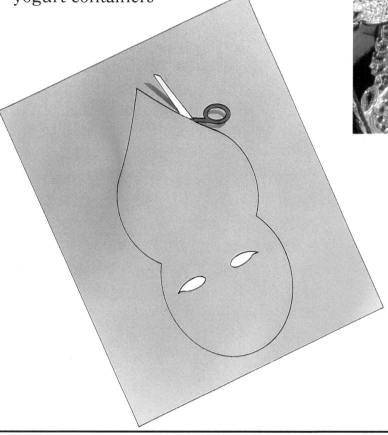

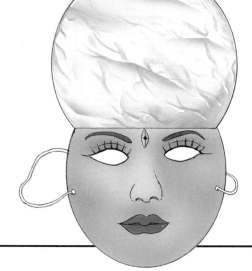

1 Draw on the cardboard an oval shape to fit your face, and above this draw a spade with a curved point at the top. Cut out the whole shape, and cut eyeholes in the face part. You could make an enlarged photocopy of the shape shown on the bottom left of page 32, then trace it onto the cardboard.

2 Paint and decorate the face of the mask, covering the top part with tinfoil. Pierce holes at the sides with scissors and tie the elastic through each hole.

3 With the masking tape, attach the wooden dowels at regular intervals to the back of the tinfoil headdress part of the mask.

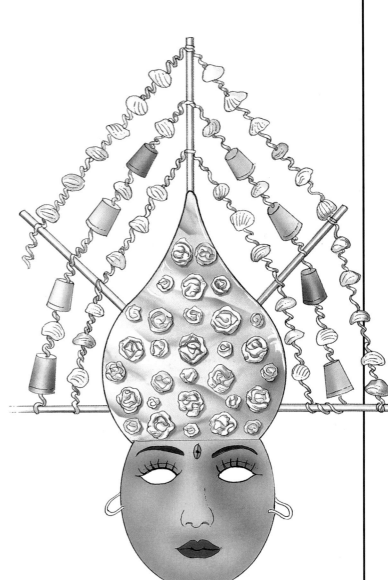

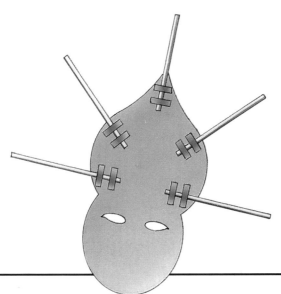

4 Turn the mask to the front again. Tie the tinsel on your first dowel rod, then wind it around the next dowel, and then the next, and so on. Then go back again, until you have gone backwards and forwards three times. Tie the tinsel at the end. Glue all your recycled materials and glitter onto the tinsel and the tinfoil parts of the headdress.

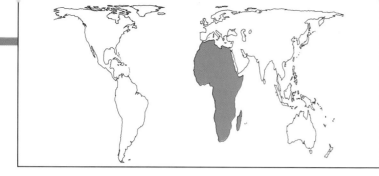

Africa

The vast African continent is home to many different peoples, each with its own way of life and language. There is a great variety of African masks. The designs and materials reflect the regions from which they come. The use of natural materials – cowrie shells, wood, raffia, animal skins, and barkcloth – is part of the African masking tradition, and the wood carving is extremely skillful. It has been said that masks were as important to Africa as cathedrals were to Europe.

These masks are worn ▶ by the Yoruba people of Nigeria during the *gelede* masquerade, in which the powerful life-force of women is celebrated.

Main picture: Masks in Africa often depict animals. This man from the Dogon people of Mali is wearing a mask representing a lizard.

Mask makers are important to African society. Traditional rules about mask-making are often handed down to younger people from elders in the community. In some cases, the tree from which a wooden mask is made has to be blessed first, so as not to offend powerful spirits. Also, some mask carvers have to work alone when making a mask, while others carve their masks in public, going to a secluded place only when the mask is ready to be covered with animal skin.

The Yoruba, who live in southwest Nigeria and Dahomey, are the largest group of people in Africa. They use wooden masks in many of their masquerades. The *gelede* masquerade is performed to ensure that the community remains healthy and wealthy. Through dance

▲ **The Dogon people of Mali wear these huge mask headdresses when performing their traditional funeral ceremony, the *dama*.**

and drama, masked figures give thanks to the "mother spirits," as they are known, which can be either creative and encouraging or angry and destructive. Some *gelede* masks have two parts, a realistic face below and a huge sculpture on top. The mask is hollowed out and rests on top of the dancer's forehead, covering the upper part of the face. The lower half of the face is covered with material. There are many traditional styles and sometimes the sculpture shows groups of figures at work or in scenes from history. More recently, rock bands, motorcycles, and women using sewing machines have been carved.

East of the Yoruba, the Obuele and Abua Igbo peoples still hold water-spirit ceremonies to appeal for good fortune. A water-spirit mask has a combination of features: partly human and partly crocodile, shark, or hippopotamus. It is large and horizontal, and when the wearer walks in water during the ceremony, the mask appears to float on the surface.

Animal and bird masks are worn at the funeral ceremonies of the Dogon peoples of Mali. All Dogon men become members of a masked dancing society called *Ava*. A few years after the death of a respected village member, a funeral ceremony called a *dama* is held.

Funerals are seen by the Dogon as a time to celebrate the joy of living, rather than the sadness of death. During the procession, the performers act out a ritual in which they pretend to take the soul of the dead person and throw it beyond the village limits. It is believed that the soul will find its way to join other dead family members.

This is a mask from the ▶ Ivory Coast. In Africa, masks often represent animal spirits.

These "tree" masks from ▶ West Africa are some of the tallest in the world. Balancing one of these masks while dancing is quite a skill.

The performers at a *dama* wear wooden rectangular masks representing reptiles, birds, and animals, which have two large, square eyeholes. A special black and white *kanaga* mask is also worn. It has a tall blade coming from its top, which can be over six feet high. During the funeral procession, the dancer sometimes bends to touch the ground with the tip of this blade.

Masked societies like the Dogon's are an important part of the African way of life. The one masking tradition in which only women participate is an initiation ceremony. It is found in Sierra Leone, Liberia, and the Ivory Coast. Here, women of the Mende peoples belong to a secret society known as the *Sande*, which is equivalent to a men's secret society called *Poro*. The *Sande* is responsible for the initiation of young girls through the different stages or grades into womanhood. Young girls are taken by the society officials to a quiet place away from the community. At various visits, the girls learn about different topics: child care, craft skills, sexual matters, and singing and dancing. Graduation ceremonies are held when the initiates return after each visit. The officials wear beautiful *sowei* masks and celebrate through dance and drama.

Sowei masks are called pot or helmet masks, as they fit completely over the wearer's head and rest on the shoulders. They are made from the trunk of a large tree, which is rubbed with palm oil until it is dark and shiny. The carving on the masks show the Mende's idea of true beauty: a small face, high, rounded forehead, elaborate hairstyle, and rolls of fat around the neck, which symbolize wealth. A long raffia costume falls from the mask, covering the whole body, and the dancers move gracefully, communicating only through movement.

Masquerades are also used as a way of making sure there is a good harvest. A British religious song, "Lord of the Dance," is based on a masquerade performed by the Senufo peoples from the Ivory Coast. The dance praises their gods for the successful sowing of seeds and asks for the rains to come. All of the Senufo spirits are carved in the wooden masks. Each mask is sacred and is worn by a specially chosen person from the village.

Masks with delicate, detailed patterns and ornaments using natural materials are still found all over Africa. The Bambara's *n'tomo* mask, modeled on a human face, is worn during ceremonies to prevent illness. It is covered with hundreds of tiny cowrie shells, beads, and dried seeds. However, manufactured materials are also having an influence on mask-making. Traditionally, the Chokwe peoples of Zaire and Angola made their fearsome caricature masks from barkcloth, the distorted features being painted on in white clay. Today, such masks are made from old burlap and brown paper.

Masks from the Chokwe people of Zaire are traditionally made of barkcloth painted with white clay.

◀ Cowrie shells are often used in African mask-making.

In Africa today, many people ▲ continue the masking tradition by wearing miniature mask jewelry.

All African masks, however simple, are an important part of African life and are treated with respect. In fact, the beautifully polished, black wooden masks of the Dan Nation of Liberia are believed to actually *be* the spirits that live in the mountainside. If a mask is put in the wrong place, it is believed to frown to show its annoyance. Masking traditions are very much alive today, and are being revived more and more as tourists want to experience the different masquerades of such varied peoples.

The importance of masks is also shown by the way many people wear tiny miniature masks as jewelry or buttons. Usually made of precious metals, clay, or wood, they are often given to a bride by her family on her wedding day as a token of good luck.

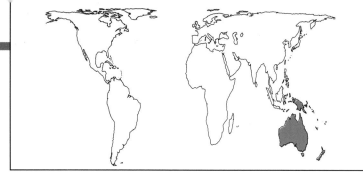

The Pacific

The islands of Melanesia in the South Pacific are the only places in that part of the world that are well known for their masks. These include souvenir masks, dance masks, and ancestor spirit masks. There are many remote areas where people still live in a traditional way, following ancient customs involving masks. Although many masks are now produced for tourists by a growing mask-making industry, these modern craftspeople still produce masks in traditional styles.

For thousands of years, masking traditions in Melanesia have been an important part of everyday life. Dance masks were once exchanged between different groups during masquerades. Ancestor spirit masks are still worn by some peoples at traditional feasts and rituals. The masks represent these powerful spirits, which have the ability to be helpful or harmful. The masks assist people to communicate with the spirits, in order to ask for help or to show respect.

Many different materials ▶
were used to make these
Pacific masks.

40

For many years, people have formed special clans, like secret societies, that try to control the power of the spirit world. Members of the clan also make sure that nonmembers behave properly toward the spirits – especially women and children, who are excluded from the clan. Only men can design, make, and wear the masks. Clan members honor their ancestors at special feasts, which are also a time when boys and young men are initiated into the adult life of the clan.

In the Sepik River valley, on the island of Papua New Guinea, masking traditions take place around the men's spirit houses, which are called *tambaran*. There is an enormous variety of masks, with each village having its own style. The most sacred masks are stored in these huge thatched buildings, which have a dance floor nearby. Dancers wear a large, cone-shaped body shroud called a *tumbuan*, representing spirits from the creation of the world. The shroud covers the face and body and has two holes at the sides for the arms. Masks of wood or clay depicting mythical ancestors, called *mwai*, are attached to the cone. Some are carved with the tongue sticking out or with gnashing teeth, designed to drive off evil spirits. *Tumbuans* are also used to warn women and children away from an important ceremonial site, or to stop them from eating coconuts being grown for a feast.

In the Maprik and Wosera areas of Papua New Guinea, enormous yams, some weighing more than 400 pounds, are kept in the spirit houses. They are grown especially for ceremonial feasts called *sing sing*. After a successful harvest they are decorated with masks in honor of the spirits of the yam harvest. The masks are made from woven rattan painted in bands of bright colors: red, yellow, black, white, and green. The larger masks are worn by dancers, and the smaller masks (less than 12 inches high) are used to decorate the yams.

Gable masks are carved in the river areas of the Middle Sepik, the Middle Ramu, and the Blackwater Lakes. Large masks made from a variety of leaves, wood, and woven cane represent female clan spirits. They are placed on house gables to protect people from disaster, especially illness. It is believed that gable masks are based on a much earlier custom of remodeling human skulls obtained by headhunting.

In the Papuan Gulf of New Guinea, an *avoko* mask is used to celebrate marriage. This small, round mask has realistic eyes and teeth, and is decorated with seeds and shells. After a husband has brought his wife home for the first time, a clan elder wears the mask in a dance, performed in front of the house, to bring the couple good luck and many children.

Pacific masks are made from all kinds ▶ **of animal and plant materials. This miniature mask is made from a turtle shell with cassowary feathers, cowrie shells, and fibers from the raffia palm tree.**

▲ A masked dancer at a ceremonial *sing sing* feast in Papua New Guinea. The mask is surrounded with fine feathers and is painted in sharp bands of color.

In Papua New Guinea souvenir masks are very common. They are miniature faces, often made of clay or turtle shell, decorated with tiny shells and small tufts of bark. They were once carved into everyday objects, such as canoe paddles, adze handles, house timbers, and drums. Today they are often given as gifts or sold to tourists.

Tortoiseshell masks from the small islands of the Torres Straits have a complicated design. They are made of pieces of tortoiseshell, sliced and cut into shapes that are then sewn together with braided coconut fiber. These are long masks, often made to look like a strange crocodile-fish creature. They were once worn at the annual *horiomu* initiation rituals, when boys and young men learned about the clan, and dancers performed pantomime in front of a screen hung with shells, skulls, and statues.

43

The Fire Dancing Mask is worn by the Baining people from the east of the island of New Britain. This fantastic mask is made of barkcloth sewn onto a rattan frame, with large ears, brightly painted eyes of red and black, and an open mouth. It is worn tilted back at an angle so the dancer can see through the mouth, and is intended to drive away evil spirits thought to be dangerous to growing children.

In the north of the island of New Ireland, the *Malanggan* ceremonies use masks called *tatanua*. People commemorate the death of a chief, some time after he has died, with a second burial ceremony. This marks the building of a new *Malanggan* house, and is also a time for initiation. These ceremonies are very competitive, as each clan tries to have more pigs and yams than there were at the last feast. During this period the young men and boys stay away from the village, but at the final feast they return wearing the *tatanua* mask.

Tatanua masks are very fierce looking, with lifelike eyes made of snail shells. They have carved wooden faces stained red, black, and white, and a high, curved headdress, made of plant fibers, barkcloth, or modern cloth, stiffened with white chalk. Sticks, seeds, or other twisted fibers are secured into a series of panels reaching up to a high crest, like the helmet of a Roman centurion or the head of a fabulous bird.

The fearsome *tatanua* mask has lifelike ▶ eyes.

Melanesian masks were traditionally made using stone axes and adzes, and skins of lizards and sharks or coral and shell were used to smooth the surfaces. Some were then coated with a mixture of clay, burnt lime, and tree oil, while others were polished with a pig's tusk or simply painted. Traditionally, natural pigments were used: lime for white, charcoal for black, soapstone for gray, ochres for yellow and brown, and plants for red and blue. Today masks are decorated with modern dyes and paints.

Masks can completely disguise the identity of the wearers. But a close look at traditional masks can reveal all sorts of things about the wearers and their customs. Next time you wear a mask to a costume party or for Halloween, remember that you are carrying on a tradition that is about 10,000 years old.

If you are making your own mask, ▶ you could use yarn for the hair.

Glossary

Adze – A cutting tool with an arched blade at a right angle to the handle.

Alderbark – Bark from an alder tree.

All Hallows' Eve – October 31, the day before All Saints' Day. It is also called Halloween.

Amazon Basin – A vast area of land stretching out from the Amazon River.

Amerindian – The first people to live in Central and South America, before the arrival of Europeans.

Amphitheater – A theater with rows of seats built one above another.

Ancestors – One's relatives from the distant past.

Archaeologists – Scientists who study the remains of ancient civilizations.

Barkcloth – Cloth made from tree bark.

Burrs – The prickly parts of certain plants.

Caribou – North American reindeer.

Caricature – An exaggerated likeness, usually of a person.

Celts – People who lived in Great Britain before the Romans.

Clan – A collection of families set apart from others and having a common ancestor.

Colonial period – A time when people from another country govern a region.

Conquistadors – Spanish and Portuguese conquerors from the early sixteenth century.

Elders – Respected older members of a community.

Epic – A very long poem about heroic deeds.

Fertility – Richness of soil, producing fruit or crops in great quantity.

Fibers – Fine strands, usually from a plant or animal, that can be made into material.

Gable – The triangular part of a wall where it meets the roof.

Gondola – A banana-shaped boat, which is the traditional form of transportation in Venice, Italy.

Gourd – A large hard-skinned fruit.

Hispanic – Describing Spanish or Spanish-speaking peoples.

Initiation – A special ceremony; for example, a ceremony to mark the time when a child becomes an adult.

Lent – The 40 days before Easter, when Christians go without certain foods or other favorite things in memory of Jesus Christ.

Manufactured – Made by machine, often used to describe something made in a factory on a large scale.

Masquerade – A performance of dancers disguised by masks.

Medieval – Having to do with a period of history known as the Middle Ages (from about the sixth to the sixteenth centuries).

Migrants – People who move from one part of the world to another.

Migration – The movement of a group of people from one part of the world to another.

Mother-of-pearl – Smooth shiny shell from an oyster.

Mythical – Existing only in myths (ancient traditional stories about gods or heroes).

Ochres – Mixtures of clay and iron products, such as iron oxide.

Pigments – Colors made from natural things, such as plants and soils.

Professionals – People who are paid for their work.

Rattan – Cane made from the thin stems of a palm tree.

Reb seeds – Seeds from an exotic African plant.

Renaissance – A period of new art and learning. In history this period came in the sixteenth century, after the Middle Ages.

Ritual – A series of actions that are always repeated at traditional ceremonies.

Sacred – Having special importance, often linked with a religious belief.

Secret Society – A clan-like group of people with secret rules and knowledge.

Shaman – A much-respected person with special powers and knowledge of the spirit world.
Shroud – A long piece of material covering the body.
Spanish Conquests – The 16th-century invasion of Spanish armies in Central and South America.
Stenciled – Decorated using cutout patterns.
Trance – A dream-like state.
Tricorn – A three-cornered hat.
Varnished – Painted with a hard shiny lacquer.

Books to Read

Gelber, Carol. *Masks Tell Stories*. Beyond Museum Walls. Brookfield, CT: Millbrook Press, 1993.

Pryor, Nick. *Putting on a Play*. New York: Thomson Learning, 1994.

Rosen, Mike. *Summer Festivals*. Seasonal Festivals. New York: Bookwright Press, 1991.

Sensier, Danielle. *Costumes*. Traditions Around the World. New York: Thomson Learning, 1995.

Russon, Jacqueline. *Face Painting*. New York: Thomson Learning, 1994.

Wright, Lyndie. *Masks*. Fresh Start. New York: Franklin Watts, 1990.

Information about individual cultures may also be found in the 48-volume Cultures of the World series by Marshall Cavendish Corporation (North Bellmore, NY), or in your library's encyclopedia.

Index

The masks in this book come from many different peoples, represent many things, and are used in all sorts of ways. The "masks" entry in this index lists the main mask designs. If you want to see how masks are used, look at the "ceremonies," "dramas," and "dances" entries. You can use the "peoples" entry to look up masks from each of the cultures mentioned in the book. If you are making a mask and you need some ideas for things to use, look at the "materials" section.